EXPLORING SPACE

THE SUN

WRITTEN BY E.C. ANDREWS

Gareth Stevens
PUBLISHING

Please visit our website, www.garethstevens.com. For a free color catalog of all our high-quality books, call toll free 1-800-542-2595 or fax 1-877-542-2596.

Published in 2025 by
Gareth Stevens Publishing
2544 Clinton St.
Buffalo, NY 14224

Written by:
E.C. Andrews

Edited by:
Noah Leatherland

Designed by:
Ker Ker Lee

Cataloging-in-Publication Data

Names: Andrews, E.C.
Title: The sun / E.C. Andrews.
Description: Buffalo, NY : Gareth Stevens Publishing, 2025. | Series: Exploring space | Includes glossary and index.
Identifiers: ISBN 9781482468724 (pbk.) | ISBN 9781482468731 (library bound) | ISBN 9781482468748 (ebook)
Subjects: LCSH: Sun--Juvenile literature.
Classification: LCC QB521.5 A537 2025 | DDC 523.7 --dc23

This edition is published by arrangement with Booklife Publishing

Printed in the United States of America

CPSIA compliance information: Batch #CW25GS: For further information contact Gareth Stevens at 1-800-542-2595.

Find us on

Photo Credits – Images are courtesy of Shutterstock.com. With thanks to Getty Images, Thinkstock Photo and iStockphoto.

Recurring images – Vector Tradition. Cover – Lukasz Pawel Szczepanski. 2–3 – Vadim Sadovski. 4–5 – muratart, WinWin artlab. 6–7 – Lukasz Pawel Szczepanski, Vadim Sadovski. 8–9 – Ed Connor, Nazarii_Neshcherenskyi. 10–11 – M.Aurelius, Mopic. 12–13 – Aphelleon, Withan Tor. 14–15 – ROZOVA SVETLANA, yanikap. 16–17 – E Forafontova, muratart. 18–19 – Simon Bratt, yanikap. 20–21 – IgorZh, SP rabbito. 22–23 – Triff, Vadim Sadovski.

CONTENTS

Words that look like this can be found in the glossary on page 24.

WHAT IS SPACE?

Space is what we call the area outside of Earth. Many scientists believe that space is infinite. This means it goes on forever. However, nobody knows for sure. Space is full of so many fascinating things.

Space is home to the solar system. The solar system is full of planets, including Earth. In the middle of our solar system is the sun. The sun is one of the most important things there.

WHAT IS THE SUN?

The sun is a star. The sun's gravity pulls smaller things toward it. This is called a gravitational pull. The sun's gravitational pull holds our solar system together.

Gravity is the force that pulls us toward the ground.

The sun looks like a big ball of fire. However, it is much hotter than any campfire found on Earth! The middle of the sun is over 27 million degrees Fahrenheit (15 million degrees Celsius)!

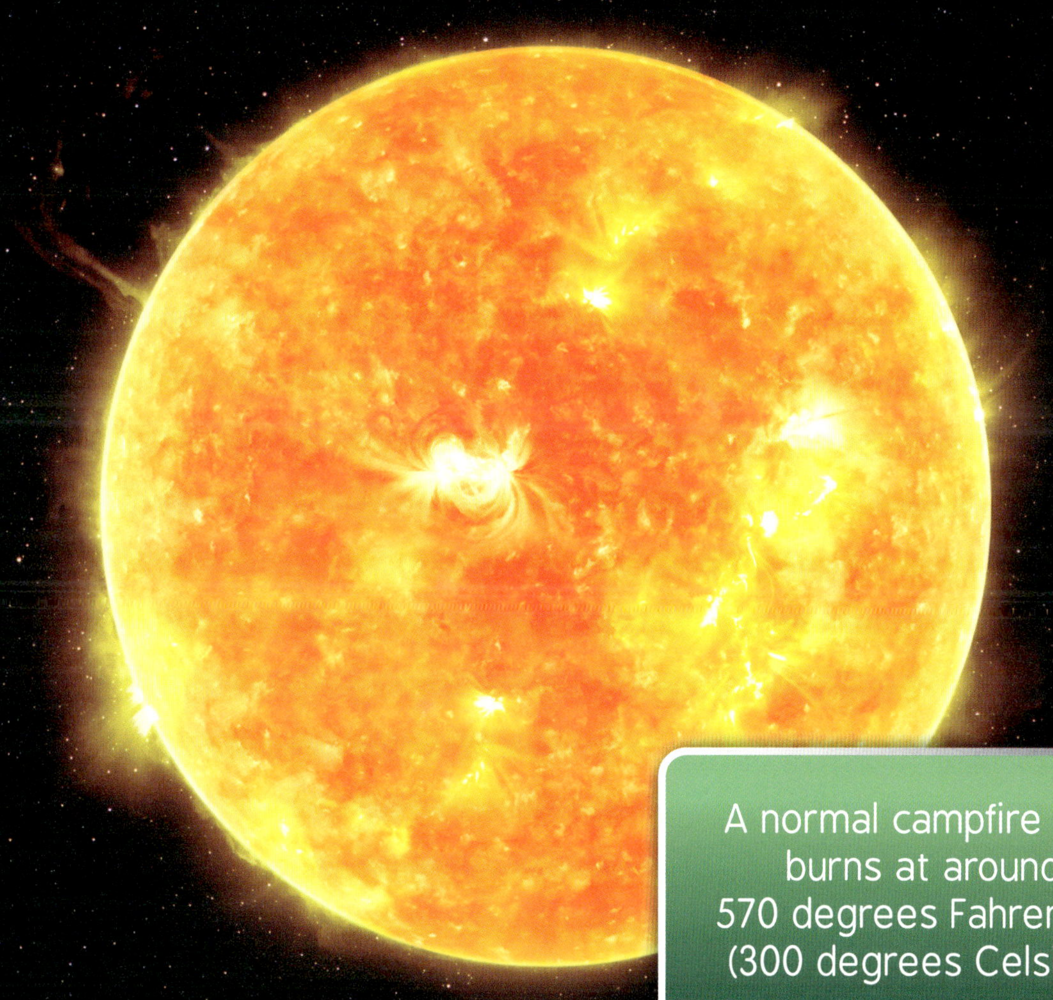

A normal campfire only burns at around 570 degrees Fahrenheit (300 degrees Celsius).

A SPECIAL STAR

There are many kinds of stars. The sun is a yellow dwarf star. Yellow dwarf stars are not the biggest type of star. However, they are much brighter than most other kinds of stars.

Although the sun is called a yellow dwarf star, it is not actually yellow. The sun is white, but Earth's atmosphere makes it look yellow from Earth.

HOW WAS THE
SUN CREATED?

The sun is around four and a half billion years old. Before the sun existed, there was a huge cloud of gas and dust. This cloud was called a nebula.

Gravity pulled this nebula inward, until it became a star. This star is now called the sun. The sun's gravity pulled other things toward it. This was the beginning of the solar system.

ORBITS

An orbit is like an invisible pathway that some objects in space follow around larger objects. This happens because of the gravitational pull of the larger object.

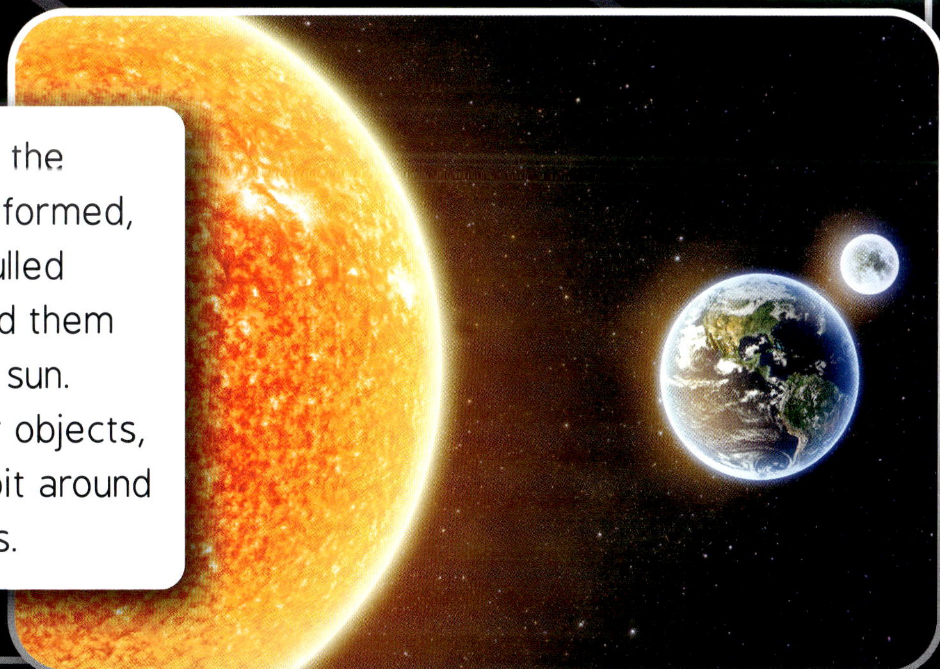

After the planets in the solar system were formed, the sun's gravity pulled them in. This caused them to orbit around the sun. Meanwhile, smaller objects, such as moons, orbit around some of the planets.

LIGHT AND HEAT

It takes around eight minutes for the sun's light and heat to reach Earth. Most living things need sunlight to stay healthy. Plants need sunlight to grow. If the sun disappeared, Earth would be completely dark.

The heat given off by the sun is the reason Earth is warm enough to live on. Without the sun, everything would be frozen. This includes all the water, which living things need to survive.

TIME

The way people track time is based on the way Earth moves around the sun. It takes just over 365 days for Earth to orbit around the sun. This is why most years are 365 days.

Earth spins on an axis. It takes around 24 hours for Earth to finish one spin. This spin is why you see the sun rise in the morning and set at night.

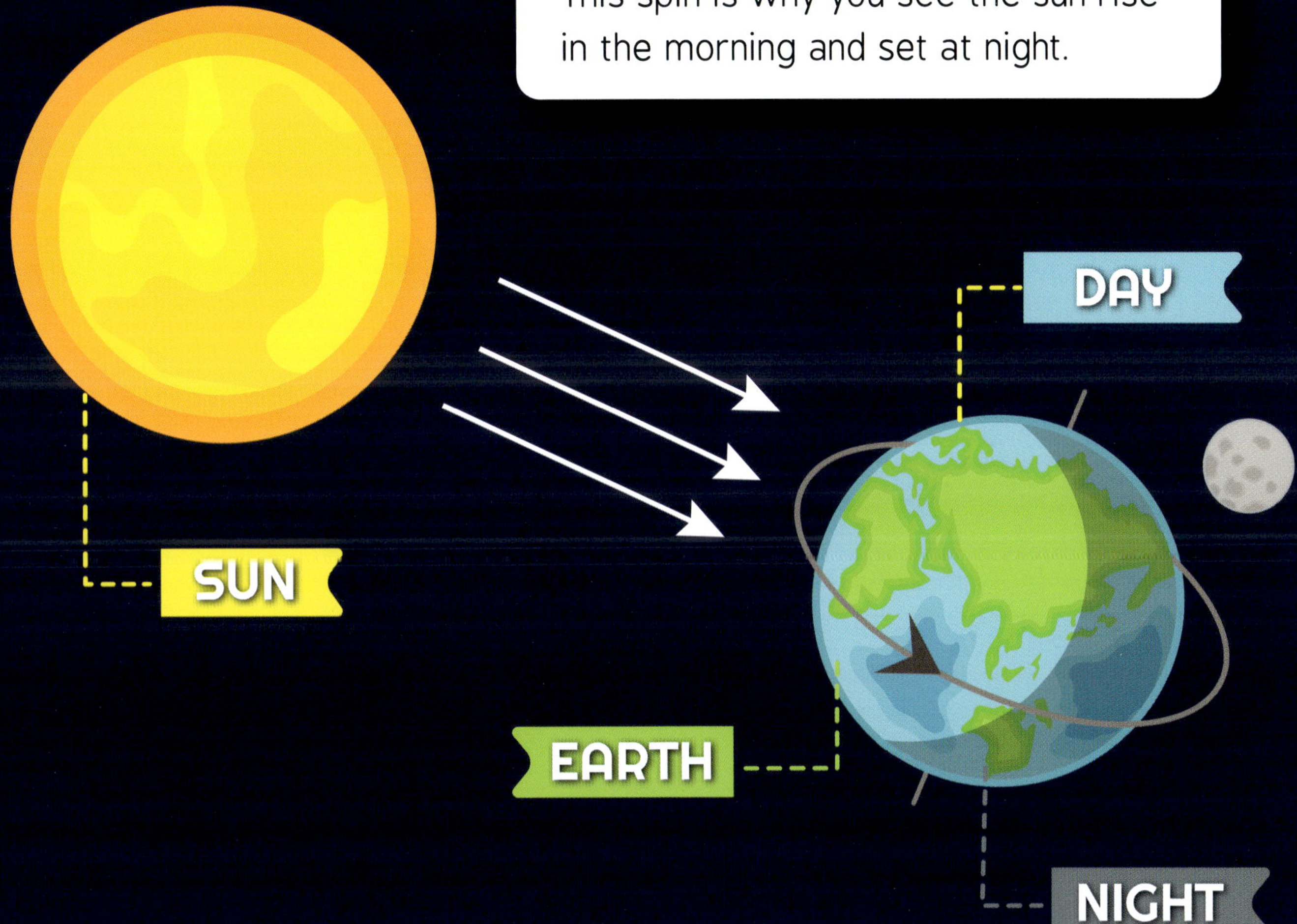

SEASONS

Earth spins on a slight tilt. This creates seasons. It is summertime on the side of Earth that is tilted towards the sun. On the other side, it is wintertime. Seasons change as Earth spins.

Some parts of the world have longer and hotter seasons because they spend more time facing the sun. Some colder parts of the world spend more time facing away from the sun.

ECLIPSES

A solar eclipse happens when the moon moves between Earth and the sun. The moon blocks the sunlight and casts a shadow onto Earth. A solar eclipse can make daytime dark.

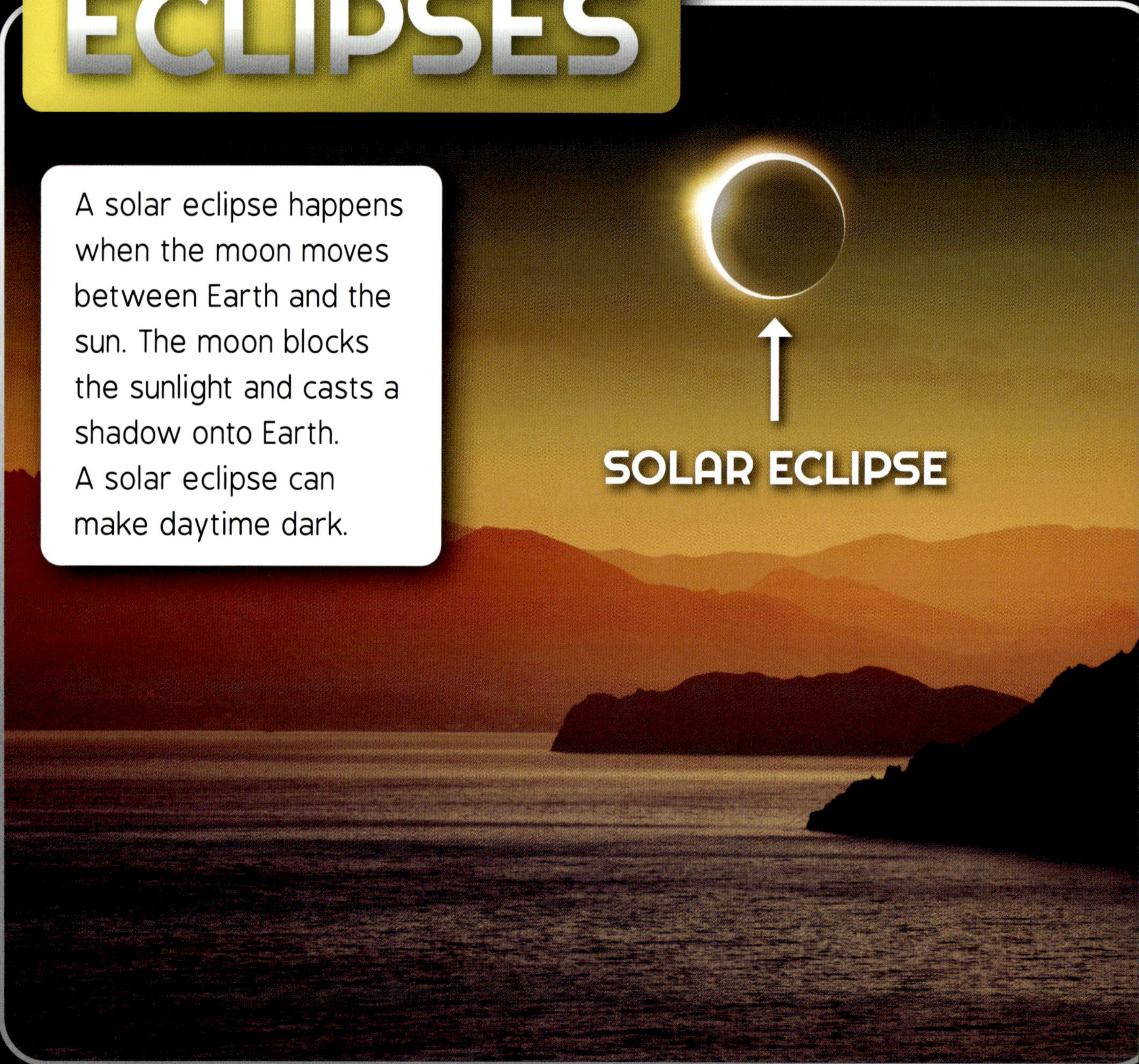

A lunar eclipse is when the moon and sun are on opposite sides of Earth. Earth's shadow stops the moon from reflecting light from the sun. Most eclipses only last for a short time.

The sun is right in the middle of the solar system. It holds all the planets in the solar system in place. Here on Earth, living things need the sun to survive.

The sun is just one part of space. From the solar system and beyond, there is so much to discover! Which part of space will you explore next?

GLOSSARY

atmosphere	the mixture of gases that make up the air and surround a planet
axis	an imaginary line that something turns on
degrees Fahrenheit	a scale of temperature where water freezes at 32 degrees and boils at 212 degrees
gas	a thing that is like air, which spreads out to fill any space available
reflecting	bouncing back light, heat, or sound
solar system	a system that includes a star and everything that orbits that star, such as planets and moons
survive	to stay alive

INDEX